GROSS-OUT CAKES

THE KITTY LITTER CAKE AND OTHER CLASSICS

Barlow • Schetselaar

Design and Photography by Amy Orton

Silverleaf Press Books are available exclusively
through Independent Publishers Group.

For details write or telephone
Independent Publishers Group, 814 North Franklin St.
Chicago, IL 60610, (312) 337-0745

Silverleaf Press
8160 South Highland Drive
Sandy, Utah 84093

Reprinted 2008

TABLE OF CONTENTS

Parents: Instructions listed in italic print involve heat, food coloring, or have a higher difficulty level and should only be done with close parent supervision.

KITTY LITTER CAKE

Difficulty: 3 Worms
Grossness: 5 out of 5 worms
Serves: 24

Ingredients

1 spice or German chocolate cake mix (18.25 oz/517g)

1 white cake mix (18.25 oz/517g)

1 large package vanilla instant pudding mix (5.9 oz/167g)

Ingredients to prepare cake & pudding mixes

1 package vanilla sandwich cookies (32 oz/907g)

Green food coloring

12 small Tootsie Rolls

Utensils

Cake pans

Various sizes of bowls

Microwave-safe dish

1 new kitty litter pan

1 new pooper scooper

Directions

1. *Prepare both cake mixes according to package instructions, using any* size pans.

2. Prepare the pudding mix according to package instructions. Refrigerate until needed.

3. *In food processor or blender, crush sandwich cookies a couple at a time. Remove crumbs before crushing more. Repeat until all are crushed.*

4. Set aside ¼ cup of the crumbs. *Add a few drops of green food coloring to the ¼ cup of cookie crumbs that you have set aside.* Mix until completely colored.

5. When cakes have cooled, crumble them into a large bowl. Gently toss in chilled pudding and half of cookie crumbs. Mix only until the cakes are moist. Pour mixture into clean litter box.

6. *Put 3 unwrapped Tootsie Rolls in a microwave-safe dish and heat until soft (probably about 10 seconds).* Shape the Tootsie Rolls to look like cat poop. Bury in the mixture. Repeat with 3 more.

7. Scatter the remaining half of the cookie crumbs over the top of the cake. Sprinkle the green crumbs on top of that. The green is supposed to look like the chlorophyll in kitty litter.

8. *Heat the remaining 6 Tootsie Rolls in the microwave.* Shape and place on top of the cake. Sprinkle with crumbs. If desired, hang one of the "poops" over the side of the kitty litter box. Serve.

step 4

step 5

Difficulty: 4
Grossness: 5
Serves: 12

DUMPSTER JUICE JUBILEE

Utensils
Small saucepan
Medium bowl
Bundt pan
Serving platter

Ingredients
¾ cup heavy (whipping) cream
1⅓ cup (8 oz/228g) semisweet
 chocolate chips
1 teaspoon pure vanilla extract
1 chocolate cake mix (18.25 oz/517g)
1 large vanilla instant pudding mix (5.9 oz/167g)

1 small chocolate instant pudding
 mix (3.4 oz/96g)
Green food coloring
Gummy worms (optional)
Candy corn (optional)
Maraschino cherries (optional)

Directions

1. *Pour cream in a small saucepan over medium heat. Bring to a boil, stirring constantly.*

2. Place chocolate chips in a medium bowl. *Carefully pour the boiling cream over the chocolate.* Stir until completely melted. Add vanilla.

3. Place the mixture in the refrigerator for 20 to 30 minutes until it thickens into a spreadable consistency.

4. Mix the chocolate cake according to the directions on the package. Pour batter into greased bundt pan.

5. Spoon chocolate onto batter, setting aside ¼ cup. As the cake cooks, the

step 5

chocolate will sink into the middle and create a molten center. *Bake cake as directed on the package.*

6. Prepare all instant pudding. *Color half of vanilla pudding light green.*

7. Remove cake immediately from pan when done and place on serving platter. Pour both flavors of pudding over cake. Drizzle remaining chocolate sauce over all.

8. If desired, place gummy worms, candy corn, and maraschino cherries on cake. Serve warm.

step 6

7

Ingredients
3 tablespoons margarine or butter
1 package (10 oz/284g) regular marshmallows
6 cups chocolate pebble cereal
Red, yellow, and green food coloring
½ cup coconut
½–1 cup mini M&M baking bits
Non-stick cooking spray

Utensils
Large saucepan
Stirring spoon
Serving plate or 13" x 9" pan
Buttered spatula or waxed paper

BARF BARS

Directions
1. *Melt margarine or butter in a large saucepan over low heat.* Add marshmallows and stir until completely melted.
2. *Add 2 drops of yellow food coloring and 1 drop of red to the marshmallows.* Stir. *Continue adding coloring in the same proportions until the marshmallows have been colored orange. Remove from heat.*
3. Add the chocolate pebble cereal and the M&M baking bits. Stir until well coated.
4. Pile onto a serving plate or, for bars, use a buttered spatula or waxed paper to press mixture into a greased 13" x 9" pan.

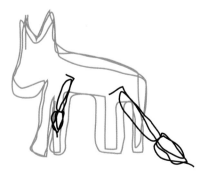

Difficulty: 2
Grossness: 4
Serves: 12

Difficulty: 4
Grossness: 3
Serves: 10

step 2

step 5

step 6

step 7

Ingredients

1 lemon cake mix (18.25 oz/517g)
1⅓ cup water
⅓ cup lemon curd
⅓ cup vegetable oil
3 large eggs
Non-stick cooking spray
1 tablespoon butter
1⅓ cup mini marshmallows
2 cup puffed rice cereal
2 large egg whites
1½ cup sugar
¼ teaspoon cream of tartar
⅓ cup water
1 teaspoon vanilla
Yellow food coloring
¼ cup powdered sugar

Utensils

Large mixing bowl
Electric mixer
9" x 13" cake pan
Cake board or platter
Medium saucepan
Large pan
Frosting spatula
Small toy dog

Directions

1. *Preheat the oven to 350°F (177°C).*

2. Mix the cake mix, water, lemon curd, oil, and eggs in a large mixing bowl. Beat the ingredients with an electric mixer until the ingredients are well blended.

3. Spray the pan with non-stick cooking spray. Pour the batter into the cake pan and *bake for 20 to 25 minutes, or until cake is golden.* Let cool. Remove from pan and place on platter or cake board.

4. To make a snowman, *melt butter and marshmallows in a medium saucepan over low heat, stirring continuously.* When melted, *remove from heat* and add puffed rice cereal.

5. Spray your hands with non-stick cooking spray. Shape the mixture into three balls—a larger for the base, medium for the body, and a smaller ball for head. Stick together and place on cake.

6. To make frosting combine egg whites, sugar, cream of tartar, and water in a pan that is not on the stove.

5. Beat on high for 1 minute with an electric mixer.

6. *Place the pan over heat and beat mixture on high speed for 7 minutes until frosting becomes stiff.*

7. Remove pan from heat. Add vanilla. Beat for 2 minutes longer on high. Take out ¼ cup frosting and add 2 drops food coloring.

8. Frost cake. Build a few peaks and valleys so frosting looks like drifting snow. Sprinkle cake with thin layer of powdered sugar.

9. Add a small toy dog near the yellow spots. Place a small piece of brownie or Tootsie Roll under dog if desired.

NEVER EAT YELLOW SNOW

Difficulty: 2
Grossness: 3
Serves: 4

PUTRID PUS POCKETS

Utensils
Cookie sheet
Tablespoon
Medium bowl
Electric mixer
Small bowl
Spoon
Paring knife

Ingredients
One 8 oz (227g) package of refrigerated crescent dinner rolls
4 oz (114g) cream cheese
1 tablespoon powdered sugar
¼ cup apricot preserves
Green food coloring
1 egg white

step 4

Directions

1. *Preheat the oven to 375°F (190°C).*
2. Open the package of dinner rolls and place on cookie sheet. Separate into 4 rectangles. Each rectangle should be made of 2 pre-cut triangles pinched together in the middle.
3. Sprinkle 1 tablespoon of powdered sugar across rectangles.
4. Whip 4 oz cream cheese (or half an 8 oz package) for 1½ minutes in a medium bowl with an electric mixer.
5. Separate the whipped cream cheese into 4 sections and put one section on each of the dough rectangles.
5. Measure apricot preserves into a small bowl and *stir in three drops of food coloring.* Preserves should become a pus-colored shade of green. Add more coloring if needed.
6. Divide the preserves up into 4 sections and spoon a section into each of the rectangles.
7. Fold the two shorter sides of the rectangle into the middle. Pinch together the open sides to completely enclose cream cheese and preserves.
7. On the top of pocket, cut an X with paring knife. Peel back points so the pockets look like open sores.
8. *Bake the pockets for 10–15 minutes until the edges are slightly brown.*

step 6

step 7

PHLEGMBRULEE

Difficulty: 4
Grossness: 4
Serves: 8

Ingredients

1 cup whole milk
2¾ teaspoons unflavored gelatin
2–3 drops green food coloring
6 tablespoon sugar
Pinch of salt
3 cup heavy cream
2 teaspoon vanilla

For Caramel Sauce

½ cup butter
1 cup brown sugar
¼ cup white corn syrup
⅛ teaspoon salt
⅛ teaspoon baking soda
⅛ teaspoon cream of tartar

Utensils

2 medium saucepans
Stirring spoon
Large measuring cup
8 half-cup ramekins
Large baking sheet
Plastic wrap
Shallow bowl
8 small serving plates

Directions

1. Pour milk into a medium saucepan and sprinkle gelatin over top. Let stand for 10 minutes.

2. *Heat milk and gelatin over high heat for about 1½ minutes, stirring constantly, until the mixture is very warm but not boiling. Remove from heat.*

3. Stir in sugar and salt. Continue stirring until dissolved, about 1 minute. Still stirring, add cream, vanilla, and food coloring.

4. Pour mixture into a large measuring cup or pitcher and pour into eight ½ cup ramekins set on a large baking sheet. Cover baking sheet with plastic wrap and refrigerate for at least 4 hours.

5. *To serve, pour 1 cup boiling water into shallow bowl. Dip the ramekin bottom into water for 3 seconds. Then, using a knife dipped in water, run knife around the edge of the ramekin.*

6. Place a small plate right-side down on the ramekin and invert. Phlegm should slide out. Spoon caramel sauce over. Serve with cough drops and tissues (optional).

For Caramel Sauce

1. *Boil butter, brown sugar, and corn syrup in a medium saucepan over medium heat until sugar has dissolved.*

2. *Remove from heat* and add salt, baking soda, and cream of tartar. Stir until all ingredients are well mixed.

step 1

step 4

TARANTULA TRIFLE

Difficulty: 2
Grossness: 2
Serves: 16

Ingredients

2 pound cake loaves
2 packages (10 oz/284g)
  frozen raspberries in syrup,
  thawed
½ cup raspberry preserves
1 large (5.9 oz/167g)
  package vanilla pudding,
  prepared
1 container (8 oz/227g)
  whipped topping
3 dozen large black gumdrops

Utensils

Rolling pin
Knife
Various sizes of bowls
Large trifle dish

step 2

step 4

step 6

Directions

1. Flatten a gumdrop with a rolling pin.

2. Slice the gumdrop into thin strips and roll. These strips will become spider legs.

3. Attach eight legs to the sides of another gumdrop. Set aside. Repeat with the other gumdrops. When you layer the trifle you'll want to add the spiders to the outside of each layer so you can see them through the dish.

4. Cut the cake loaves into small rectangles and set aside.

5. Drain the raspberries and mix with preserves.

6. To layer the trifle, first put ⅓ of the cake squares in the bottom of the trifle dish and pour ⅓ of the whipped topping on top. Next spread on ⅓ of the pudding, then ⅓ of the raspberry mixture over all. Repeat until you have 3 layers of each or dish is full. Top with whipped topping and spiders.

step 2

step 4

step 5

Ingredients

1¼ cup crushed chocolate sandwich cookies

4 tablespoon melted butter or margarine

Two 8 oz packages (two 227g) cream cheese

1 can (14 oz/397g) sweetened condensed milk

3 eggs

¼ cup lemon juice

15 chocolate sandwich cookies, crushed

1 small tube yellow decorator's icing

1 can raspberry pie filling (21 oz/595g)

Utensils

9" pie pan

Electric beater

1 plastic rat or other common road kill

Directions

1. *Preheat oven to 300°F (150°C).*

2. Combine chocolate sandwich cookie crumbs and melted butter. Press into a 9" pie pan.

3. Beat the cream cheese with an electric beater until fluffy.

4. Beat in milk until smooth. Beat in eggs and lemon juice.

5. Pour mixture in pie pan and *bake for 50–55 minutes, or until the center has thickened to a solid.*

6. After cheesecake has cooled, spread crushed chocolate sandwich cookies on the cake.

7. *Pipe yellow icing in a double line on cake to look like lines on a road.*

8. Put a large spoonful of pie filling in the middle of the road and smear it to look like blood. Place plastic road kill on top, with another spoonful of pie filling on the side and top. When serving, place a spoonful of pie filling next to every piece.

ROAD KILL CHEESECAKE

Difficulty: 4
Grossness: 4
Serves: 8

Difficulty: 4
Grossness: 5
Serves: 20

COW
PIE
CAKE

Ingredients
2 boxes (18.25 oz/517g)
  chocolate cake mix, plus
  ingredients to prepare mix
2 cans (16 oz/454g) chocolate
  frosting, dyed dark green
½ cup peanuts
½ cup raisins
1 cup sweetened coconut flakes
10 red gummy worms
½ cup candy corn
Red and green food coloring

Utensils
4 round cake pans, any size
Serving platter or new,
  synthetic grass
Spatula

Directions

1. Prepare the cake mixes according to the package directions. Fold the raisins and peanuts into the batter.

2. Pour batter into 4 greased and floured round cake pans and *bake according to package directions. Let cool, then remove from the pans.*

3. Cut the cakes into various shapes and place on serving platter or piece of new, synthetic grass.

4. Divide the coconut into thirds. Make ⅓ brown by mixing the red and green color, and mix the last ⅔ into the frosting.

5. Push ¼ cup candy corn into the cake, spacing each piece randomly. Frost the cake in a circular pattern with a spatula dipped in water to prevent breaking the cake.

6. Sprinkle the brown coconut all over the cake and grass to look like dirt. Push the gummy worms into the cake and the remaining candy corn into the frosting. If you want more embellishment, add black plastic flies.

step 5

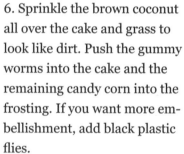

Difficulty: 3
Grossness: 3
Makes: 4 nests

BIRD BOMBED NEST

Utensils
Double boiler
Stirring spoon
Mixing bowls
Serving plates

Ingredients
1 bag (11.5 oz/326g)
 chocolate chips
⅓ cup peanut butter
3 cup chow mein noodles
1 cup whipped cream
4 marshmallow birds (or fake
 birds from craft store)
15 small marshmallows
Non-stick cooking spray

step 2

step 4

step 4

Directions
1. *Melt the bag of chocolate chips in a double boiler over medium heat, stirring frequently. Add peanut butter. Continue stirring until mixture has melted and is completely blended.*
2. *Take pan off heat.* Stir in chow mein noodles. Mix until noodles are completely covered.
3. Place mixing bowls on working surface. Spray with non-stick cooking spray.
4. Take a spoonful of mixture and begin molding it against the side of a mixing bowl with a spoon. Repeat until you have formed a nest. Let cool.
5. To remove nest from bowl, *dip the bottom of the bowl in a container of warm water,* then slide the nest out. Place on serving plates.
6. Hold a spoonful of whipped cream about 8 inches above the nest and let it splat down onto the nest for the bird droppings. Repeat few times above each nest.
7. Place a marshmallow bird in each nest with smaller marshmallows beside for eggs. You can decorate the nest by placing clean rocks and leaves on the plate. Serve.

Difficulty: 3
Grossness: 4
Serves: 12

TOENAIL TORTE WITH TOE JAM FILLING

Ingredients

Small amount of cream-colored marzipan
Non-stick cooking spray
1 caramel cake mix (18.25 oz/517g), plus
  ingredients to prepare mix
1 large package (5.9 oz/167g) vanilla instant
  pudding, plus ingredients to prepare mix
3 bananas
1 cup caramel ice cream topping

Utensils

Waxed paper
Rolling pin
Large toenail clippers, new
3 round 9-inch pans
Serving platter

Directions

1. Roll out the marzipan to toenail thickness. Set aside on waxed paper for a day, uncovered.

2. When dried, clip "toenails" with a new set of toenail clippers. Set clippings aside.

3. Spray well the sides and bottom of three 9-inch round cake pans. Prepare and *bake cake mix according package directions,* with batter evenly divided between pans. *Remove cakes from pans* and let cool on a flat surface.

4. Prepare pudding according to pie filling directions. Let set up in refrigerator for 1 hour. Slice bananas into mix.

5. Place one layer of cake on serving platter. Spread pudding on top until it's about one inch from the edge. Place second cake on top. Pudding may ooze over the edges. Repeat with other cake layers and pudding.

6. *Warm caramel topping in microwave until just pourable. Drizzle over cake.* Sprinkle toenail clippings on the caramel topping. Serve with the clippers on the side or top of the cake. Serve immediately.

step 1

step 2

step 5

25

Difficulty: 3
Grossness: 1
Serves: 12

SNAKE CAKE

Ingredients

Non-stick cooking spray
1 cup vegetable oil
4 egg whites
½ cup milk
1 package white cake mix (18.25 oz/517g)
20 chocolate sandwich cookies
1 small package (3.4 oz/96g) white
    chocolate instant pudding mix
2 cans of white frosting (two 16 oz/454g)
Food coloring
Various candies for decorating

Utensils

Bundt cake pan
Large bowl
Electric mixer
Cutting board
Chopping knife
Cooling rack
Platter or cake board
Frosting spatula

Directions

1. *Preheat oven to 350°F (177°C).* Spray bundt pan with non-stick cooking spray.

2. Combine cake mix, pudding mix, oil, egg whites, and milk in a large bowl. Beat with electric mixer at medium speed for 2 minutes, or until well blended.

3. On a cutting board, chop cookies with a chopping knife. Stir into batter.

3. Spread mixture in bundt pan. *Bake 50 to 60 minutes or until a toothpick inserted near the center comes out clean.* Cool 1 hour in pan on cooling rack.

4. Remove cake from cake pan onto a platter or cake board. Cut the cake into uneven pieces, and *assemble on serving platter in a serpentine fashion as shown in the photograph.*

5. *Dye frosting desired color.* Frost the cake with a frosting spatula dipped in water to prevent cake from breaking.

6. Use candies and frosting to decorate snake.

step 4

step 4

step 5

step 6

BLOOD CLOT CAKE

Ingredients

4 tablespoons butter
½ loaf of day-old French bread
3 eggs
2 cups milk
½ cup sugar
2 teaspoon vanilla
½ teaspoon ground cinnamon
½ teaspoon ground nutmeg
½ teaspoon salt
Red food coloring
1 cup fresh raspberries
3 tablespoon butter
2 tablespoon sugar
1 tablespoon cornstarch
¾ cup milk
¼ cup grenadine syrup
1 teaspoon vanilla

Utensils

Small, microwave safe bowl
9" x 13" glass dish
Wooden spoon
Medium mixing bowl
Whisk
Teaspoon
Toothpick
Saucepan
Small mixing bowl
Fork

Difficulty: 4
Grossness: 5
Serves: 10

Directions

1. *Preheat oven to 350°F (177°C) degrees.* Tear the French bread into 1-inch pieces. Measure 4 cups of the pieces and use them to fill the 9" x 13" dish.

2. *Place butter in small, microwave-safe bowl and melt it in the microwave for 30 seconds. Pour butter over bread pieces.* Stir with wooden spoon until the pieces are evenly coated with the butter.

3. In a medium mixing bowl, use a whisk to mix eggs, milk, sugar, vanilla, cinnamon, nutmeg, and salt. *Add red food coloring until the mixture is blood red.* Stir in raspberries.

4. Pour mixture over bread crumbs. Stir gently until mixture is evenly blended.

5. *Place casserole dish in oven. Bake for 40 minutes or until a toothpick inserted in the center comes out clean.*

6. *While cake is in the oven, melt 3 tablespoons of butter in a small saucepan.*

7. In a small mixing bowl, combine sugar and cornstarch. Mix with a fork and then add it to the melted butter. Stir in milk and grenadine syrup.

8. *Cook the mixture over medium heat until it reaches a full boil, stirring constantly. Continue stirring and boiling for one minute.*

9. *Remove from heat* and stir in vanilla. Set aside until cake is cool enough to eat.

10. To serve, cut the cake into pieces and pour warm blood sauce over each piece.

step 2

step 3

step 4

step 4

SLIME MOUSS[...]

Ingredients
1 large package (5.9 oz/167g)
 instant pudding
1½ cup thawed whipped crea[m]
Green and blue food coloring

Utensils
Large mixing bowl
3 medium bowls
Serving cups

Directions

1. Prepare the pudding according to directions on package.

2. Mix in thawed whipped cream.

3. Divide mixture into three medium-sized bowls. Dye one mixture light green, one dark green, and one blue.

4. Layer the mousse in serving cups. Refrigerate until served.

step 3   **step 4**

Difficulty 1
Grossness 2
Makes 4

DAY OLD BATH WATER

Directions

1. Thaw sherbet for approximately 15 minutes and place in tub. Add soda and prepared lemonade. The sherbet will melt to form multi-colored scum.
2. Float a handful of green, yellow, and white after dinner mints on top of the scummy punch to look like little bars of soap.

Ingredients
1 can (12 oz/340g) frozen lemonade, prepared
2 L bottle of lemon lime soda
½ gallon (2 L) rainbow sherbet
After dinner mints

Utensils
Clean plastic tub

HIDEOUS HAIRBRUSHES

Directions

1. Cut 2 Twinkies in half lengthwise. Take the flat bottom halves and turn it filling-side-down on vanity tray for a brush handle. Place a whole Twinkie at the top of the handle for the head of the brush.
2. Mix coconut with chocolate frosting. Spread on top half of Twinkies.
3. Break the top third off pretzels and discard. Stick the remaining pieces into the frosted sections of the Twinkies.
4. Wind the black licorice ropes around pretzels to look like matted hair.

Ingredients
4 Twinkies
20 small pretzel sticks
10 strands of black licorice ropes
¼ cup chocolate frosting
⅛ cup coconut

Utensils
Vanity tray

EARWAX SWABS

Directions

1. Cut the straws into 2 ½ inch pieces. Press a mini marshmallow into each end of the straws.
2. Pour butterscotch chips in a medium microwave-safe bowl. *Melt in the microwave at low power or defrost setting for about 30 seconds. Stir. Repeat process until chips are thoroughly melted.*
3. Dip ends of "swabs" into the melted butterscotch and place on wax paper to harden.

Ingredients
24 mini marshmallows
6 oz (170g) butterscotch chips

Utensils
12 solid-color, straight straws
Medium microwave-safe bowl

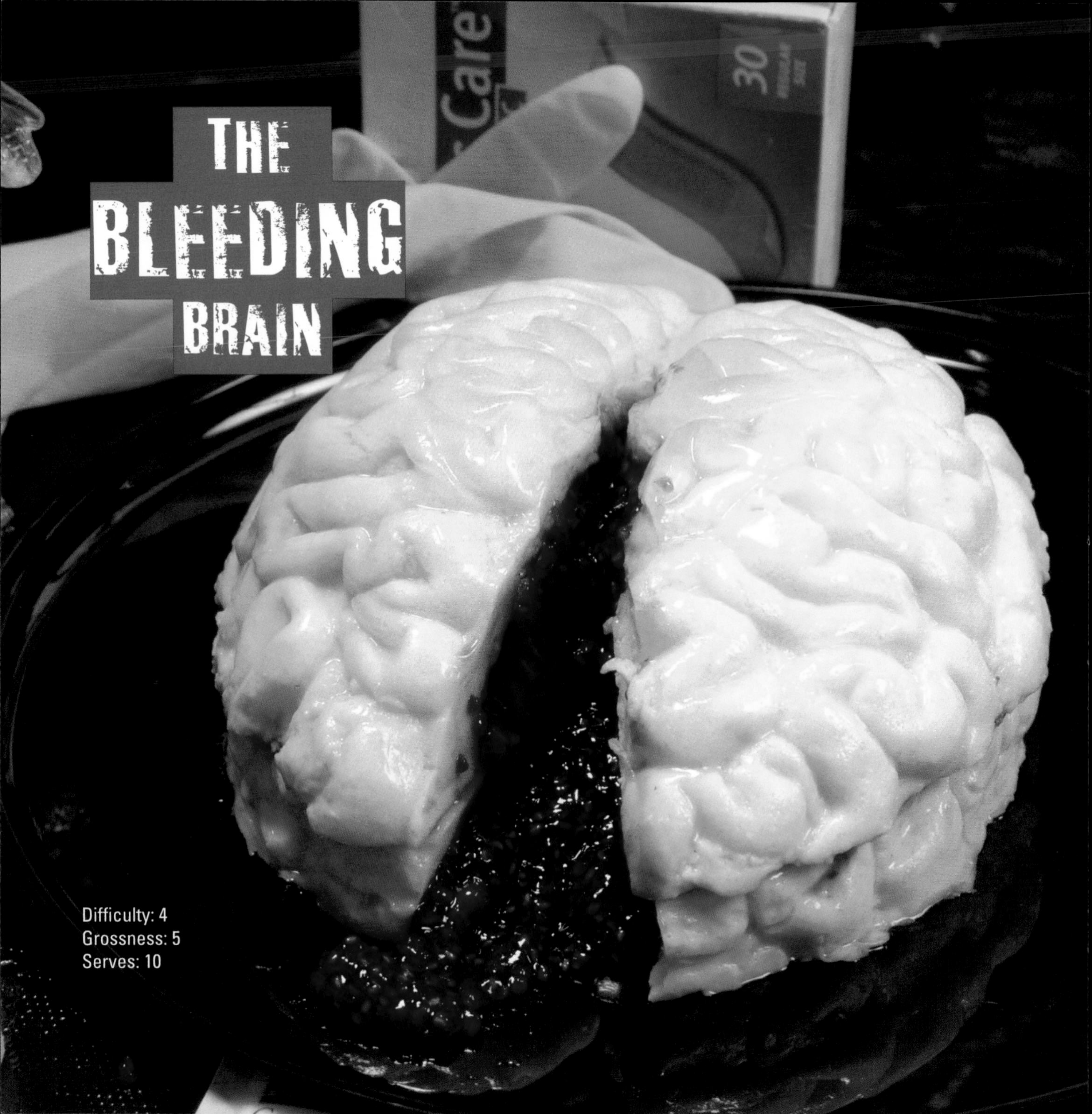

THE BLEEDING BRAIN

Difficulty: 4
Grossness: 5
Serves: 10

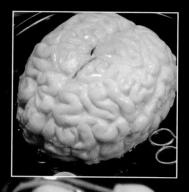

Ingredients

4 tablespoons unflavored gelatin
2 cups cold milk
1 cup heavy cream
2 cans (15 oz/425g) peaches in
 heavy syrup
6 tablespoons peach-flavored syrup
1 can (21 oz/425g) raspberry
 pie filling

Utensils

1 large gelatin brain mold (you can
 find this on many web sites)
Small saucepan
Whisk
Medium bowl
Blender

step 4

Directions

1. Pour the milk and cream into a small saucepan and sprinkle with gelatin. Whisk the mixture well, then let it sit for 3 minutes.
2. *Place the pan over medium heat and bring to a boil,* whisking frequently to insure gelatin dissolves. *Immediately remove pan from the heat and pour contents into a medium bowl.* Let the mixture cool for about 20 minutes.
3. *In a blender, puree peaches and syrup.* Add peaches to cooled cream mixture and stir. Pour half of mixture into brain mold. Chill until firm but not set—about 1–1½ minutes.
4. Remove the mold from refrigerator. Scoop out a small space in the center of the mold and fill with raspberry pie filling. *Care-*

step 4

fully pour the remaining gelatin mixture over the filling. Chill until firm, at least 4 hours.
5. *To unmold, dip mold in a bowl filled with hot water, taking care to not let any water get into the mold. Remove from water and dry outside of mold. Place serving tray over bottom of mold and carefully flip both over to remove gelatin from mold.* Store in refrigerator until ready to use.
6. Before serving, cut the brain in half and spread the halves apart so it "bleeds" onto the tray. Serve on a metal tray with surgical instruments on the side (optional).

GOOGLY EYEBALL

Ingredients

1 white cake mix (18.25 oz/517g), plus ingredients to prepare mix

Non-stick cooking spray

2 packages (two 10 oz/ 284g) frozen sweetened strawberry slices, thawed

1 container of pre-made white frosting

Food coloring for eye color

1 tube black frosting

1 tube red decorating gel

Utensils

Round metal bowl

Serving plate or platter

Skewer

Wooden spoon

Blender or food processor

step 2

step 3

step 3

Directions

1. *Preheat oven to 350°F (177°C) degrees.* Spray the inside of a round metal bowl with non-stick cooking spray.

2. Prepare the cake mix according to package instructions. *Bake in metal bowl until a skewer inserted in the middle comes out clean.*

3. Let cool. Gently remove cake from bowl and place on serving plate or platter.

3. Poke holes in top of cake 1 inch apart using the handle of a wooden spoon. *Puree thawed strawberries with juice in a blender or food processor.* Spoon mixture into holes and wipe off excess.

4. Spread frosting over the cake, removing ¼ cup.

5. Dye ¼ cup frosting color of desired iris (colored portion).

6. Frost large circle on top of cake with colored frosting. Use tube of black frosting to create a pupil in center of colored circle.

7. Use red decorating gel to create veins on the cake.

8. Pour any extra strawberry sauce around bottom of cake. Serve.

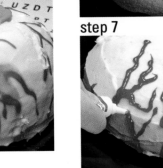

step 7

Difficulty: 3
Grossness: 4
Serves: 10

SQUEAMISH SKEWERS

Ingredients

1 package (18 oz/510g) refrigerated sugar cookie dough
½ cup flour
Whole blanched almonds (6 oz/170g)
Red food coloring
4 yellow apples
Lemon juice
1 package (10 oz/284g) frozen strawberries in syrup, thawed

step 1

Utensils

Cookie sheet
Paring knife
Apple peeler
Wooden skewers
Paper towels
Blender
Empty, clean ketchup bottle

step 2

step 7

Directions

1. Mix cookie dough with flour. Roll half of dough to ¼ inch thick.

2. Cut out finger-shaped pieces of dough. Place on greased cookie sheet.

3. Pinch in finger to create knuckles. Use wooden skewer to draw wrinkles.

4. *Paint almonds with red food coloring.* Press almond in finger to form a nail.

5. Roll other half of cookie dough to ¼ inch thick. Cut long strips and form ½ inch balls. Push two balls on each end of each strip. Flatten. Place on cookie sheet.

6. Using a wooden skewer, poke a hole in bones and fingers for skewers later. Holes must be slightly larger than skewer. *Bake cookies at 325° F (163°C) for 20- 25 minutes or until golden brown.*

7. *Cut apples into 4 quarters with a paring knife. Cut seeds out of each slice and then cut each slice in half again. Cut away half of the peel on the lower narrow end of each one and then using a knife or peeler shape a nail in the remaining peel.*

8. *Use knife to shape the apple to look like a big toe.* Squirt toes with lemon juice so they don't turn brown.

9. When the fingers have cooled enough to handle, start layering on skewers. Dry off toes with a paper towel before skewering.

10. Put the strawberries in a blender and puree. *Pour "blood" sauce in ketchup bottle* and serve on side.

39

Ingredients

1 package (18 oz/510g) refrigerated sugar
   cookie dough
1 package (8 oz/227g) cream cheese, softened
⅓ cup powdered sugar
Yellow and green food coloring
10 chocolate-covered raisin clusters
10 chocolate-covered peanut clusters
Small Tootsie Rolls (about 8)
Caramel sauce
½ cup mini M&Ms
3 vanilla sandwich cookies (optional)

Utensils
Pizza pan

Difficulty: 2
Grossness: 3
Serves: 8

Directions

1. *Preheat the oven to 350°F (177°C).* Spread cookie dough on pizza pan until it's about half an inch thick.
2. Trim off extra dough. *Bake for 18–20 minutes or until cookie is light golden brown.* Turn the oven off and let crust cool.
3. Combine cream cheese and sugar and mix well. Add about 10 drops of yellow food coloring and 1 drop green to cream cheese mixture. Spread on cooled crust.
4. Randomly place peanut and raisin clusters on pizza, then put pizza back in the oven that's been turned off. Watch carefully and remove just as the clusters start to melt, 3–5 minutes.
5. *Put 3 unwrapped Tootsie Rolls in the microwave and heat until they're soft enough to mold—about 10 seconds.* Mold into funny shapes and place them on the pizza. Do the same thing to as many other Tootsie Rolls as you would like.
6. Pour caramel sauce over pizza. Sprinkle M&Ms and crumble cookies over top as a garnish (optional). Slice and serve.

step 3

step 4

step 5

SLUDGE PILE PIZZA

DOGGIE DOO DOO DROPS

Ingredients

½ cup milk
½ cup margarine or butter
2 cup sugar
½ cup cocoa
1 cup chunky peanut butter
3 cup oats
1 teaspoon vanilla

Utensils

Medium saucepan
Large stirring spoon
Waxed paper

step 3

step 4

Directions

1. Measure milk, margarine, and sugar into medium saucepan. *Mix on medium heat.*
2. *Stir until the mixture comes to a boil. Boil for one minute, stirring continuously.*
3. *Remove from heat* and add cocoa, peanut butter, oats, and vanilla. Stir well.
4. Mold handfuls of the mixture into doggie doo doo-sized cookies. Place molded cookies on waxed paper to cool.

Difficulty: 2
Grossness: 5
Makes: 20

Difficulty: 1
Grossness: 2
Makes: 10

Ingredients

8 oz (227g) cream cheese, softened
1 cup powdered sugar
2 small packages (two 3.4 oz/96g) chocolate
    instant pudding mix
4 cups milk
1 package chocolate sandwich cookies
½ lb. (227g) gummy worms

Utensils

Mixing bowl
Electric hand mixer
2 Freezer-sized ziplock bags
Rolling pin
1 clean flower pot or
    new sand pail
Optional: garden trowel or
    fake plant

Directions

1. In mixing bowl, blend together cream cheese, powdered sugar, and pudding mix with an electric hand mixer. Gradually stir-in milk. Chill in refrigerator.

2. Place a couple of cookies in a ziplock bag. Put that bag in another bag. Crush the cookies with rolling pin. Empty the crushed cookies into a bowl and repeat until all the cookies are crushed.

3. *Line flower pot or pail with foil.*

4. To layer the cake, first pour pudding mixture into pot or pail, then add ¾ of the ground cookies, then a layer of gummy worms. Place remainder of ground cookies on top.

5. Place remainder of gummy worms emerging from soil. Optional: Serve with a garden trowel or fake plant.

step 2

step 4

step 4

BUG AND DIRT CAKE

Ingredients

1 cake mix of choice, plus ingredients to prepare
   mix (18.25 oz/517g)

20–24 cupcake liners

1 can vanilla frosting

Food coloring

Various candies

Utensils

Muffin tin

Small bowls for mixing frosting

Frosting spatula

Difficulty: 2
Grossness: 1
Makes: 20

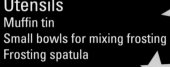

ALIEN CUPCAKES

Directions

1. Place cupcake liners inside muffin tin and *bake cupcake mix according to the package directions*. Let cool.
2. Divide frosting into small bowls and *use food coloring to dye each a different color*. Frost cupcakes using spatula.
3. Use candies to decorate the faces of your aliens in the way you wish.

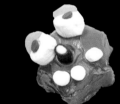

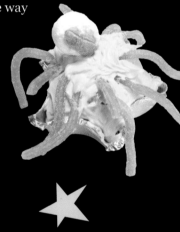

Cupcake Ideas

• Look for specialty cupcake liners if you would like your cupcakes a different shape.
• Add pizzazz to your cupcake by adding filling. Spoon a tablespoon of jam, a large berry, or chocolate candy on the top before baking. As the cupcake bakes, it will sink into the middle. You can also use a pastry bag to fill it with 1 tablespoon of pudding after it has baked.
• Use neon food coloring for brighter frosting colors.

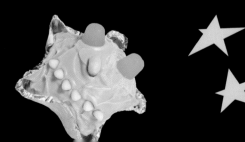

step 3

step 3

step 7

step 7

Ingredients

2 brownie mixes (20 oz/567g)
Ingredients to prepare mixes
1 can chocolate
  frosting (16 oz/454g)
10 chocolate sandwich cookies
1 cup coconut
Green food coloring
Candy rocks (optional)
Black licorice ropes
¼ teaspoon lemon extract
2 sugar cubes

Utensils

Two 8" x 13" pans
Small bowl
Food processor or
  sealable bags and rolling pin

Directions

1. *Bake brownie mixes according to the directions on the back of the box in two 8" x 13" pans.* Save one eggshell from the ingredients added.

2. While brownies are baking, thoroughly wash eggshell, inside and out. This will make the pocket for the flame. Set aside.

3. When brownies have cooled, take a handful of brownies from the second pan and begin sculpting an anthill on the first pan of brownies. Make a hole in the top and insert eggshell inside.

4. Frost the first plate of brownies and the base of the anthill. Crush the chocolate sandwich cookies in a food processor or with a rolling pin as shown on page 45, step 2. Spread crumbs on half of cake and pat onto sides.

5. Place coconut in a small bowl and *mix with a couple of drops of green food coloring.* Stir until color is evenly distributed. Sprinkle the coconut on half of cake. Add optional candy rocks to "grass."

6. Begin sculpting the ants from the second pan of brownies by creating three round balls of brownies and sticking them together. Repeat until you have 3 ants.

7. Cut pieces of licorice rope 1½" (14cm) long, six for each ant. Insert them in the center circle of ant's body. Cut two more pieces for antennae and place them in the ant's head. Repeat for other ants.

8. Place ants on the cake.

9. *To create flame, place sugar cubes in eggshell and pour lemon extract over top when ready to serve. Light sugar cubes. Best served in a darkened room.*

FLAMING
ANT CAKE

Difficulty: 3
Grossness: 3
Serves: 10

BOOGERY BUNDT

Difficulty: 4
Grossness: 4
Makes: 10

Ingredients

Angel food bundt cake (16 oz/454g)
Small package (3.4 oz/96g) vanilla pudding
Ingredients to make pudding mix
Green food coloring
1 jar (13 oz/367g) marshmallow creme
3 tablespoons sour cream
1 teaspoon vanilla extract
½ can sweetened condensed milk
2⅔ cups flaked coconut
1 small package lime gelatin (3 oz/85g)
1 cup ground blanched almonds
1 teaspoon almond extract
¾ cup flaked coconut

Utensils

Cake platter
Frosting bag with round tip
Rubber spatula
Electric mixer
Bowls
Cookie sheet
Waxed paper

step 2

step 7

step 7

step 9

Directions

1. Prepare pudding mix according to package instructions. *Spoon into assembled frosting bag.*

2. Push tip deeply into cake. Slowly squeeze bag to insert pudding inside. Stop squeezing when pudding erupts from cake's side.

3. *Remove lid from glass jar of marshmallow creme and place jar in microwave. Heat on high power for 45 seconds.*

4. With a rubber spatula, remove creme from jar into medium bowl. Add sour cream and vanilla. Beat with electric mixer on high until light and fluffy. Spoon mixture over bundt.

5. To make Booger Balls, combine sweetened condensed milk, coconut, ⅓ cup of unprepared gelatin, almonds, and almond extract in a large bowl. Mix well.

6. Cover bowl with plastic wrap and chill for about an hour or until mixture is firm enough to mold in your hands.

7. Place remainder of gelatin in a small bowl. Mold various sizes of balls from mixture and roll in gelatin. Place balls on a cookie sheet lined with waxed paper.

8. Return the cookie sheet to fridge until ready to serve.

9. When ready to serve, place booger balls around and on cake and drizzle with marshmallow. Sprinkle ¾ cup flaked coconut on top of all. Serve.

Utensils

Muffin tin
Cupcake liners
1 new, clean flyswatter

Ingredients

1 vanilla cake mix (18.25 oz/517g)
Ingredients to prepare mix
2 cups mini chocolate chips
1 can chocolate frosting (16 oz/454g)
Powdered sugar
Round chocolate candies
   with soft filling
Hard sugar-coated candies, small
1 small tube red piping gel

Directions

1. Prepare the cupcakes as directed on the package, mixing mini chocolate chips into batter before baking. Use cupcake liners. *Bake and let cool.*

2. Remove from muffin tin and place on tray or platter. Frost each cupcake. Let cupcakes sit, uncovered, for 2 hours, or until frosting is no longer sticky.

3. *Press flyswatter into frosting and sprinkle with powdered sugar. Carefully lift flyswatter when finished so it leaves imprint of swatter.*

4. Gently smash the chocolate candies in your fingers. Place at one end of the cupcake for fly's head. Press sugar-coated candies on chocolate candies for fly's eyes.

5. Pipe red gel around edge of frosting and fly's head for a just-swatted look. Serve with clean flyswatter on the side.

FOUL "FLY"ING CUPCAKES

Difficulty: 3
Grossness: 3
Serves: 20

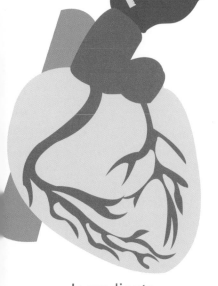

PUMPING HEART TART

Directions

1. *Boil water in a small saucepan and remove from heat.* Pour the gelatin into the water and stir until completely dissolved.

2. Spray the inside of a large teacup (the bigger the better) or round-bottomed ramekin coated with non-stick cooking spray. Fill the teacup with the gelatin and refrigerate until firm, about 3 hours.

3. Make the filling in a medium bowl by combining sweetened condensed milk, sour cream, lemon juice, vanilla, *and a couple of drops of red food coloring.* Mix well, then cover and chill for at least 40 minutes.

4. To make the crust for the tart, mix together the butter and brown sugar in second medium bowl and beat until fluffy.

5. Add flour, oats, and nuts and mix thoroughly.

6. Spray pie pan with non-stick cooking spray. Press dough into pie pan, spreading mixture to the edge.

7. *Bake at 350°F (177°C) for 10–12 minutes or until golden brown.*

8. When the crust has cooled completely, pour filling in crust. Set some licorice whips into filling to look like veins.

9. Invert the teacup or ramekin in middle of tart. *To help loosen the gelatin, place bottom of container in warm water before inverting.* Gently shake and tap the sides of the container.

10. Push the licorice whip through heart so they stick out evenly on both sides and look like major arteries. Gently push lace under the bottom of the heart. Serve.

Ingredients

¾ cup water
1 box (3 oz/85g) strawberry gelatin
1 can (14 oz/397g) sweetened condensed milk
½ cup sour cream
¼ cup lemon juice
1 teaspoon vanilla
Red food coloring
½ cup plus 1 tablespoon butter
¼ cup brown sugar
1 cup flour
¼ cup quick cooking oats
¼ cup finely chopped nuts
Red licorice whips
Red licorice laces

Utensils

Small saucepan
Stirring utensil
Large teacup or small, round-bottomed ramekin
2 medium bowls
Pie pan

step 3

step 5

step 6

step 9

Difficulty: 4
Grossness: 4
Serves: 8

Difficulty: 5
Grossness: 3
Serves: 20

step 4

step 7

step 8

step 8

Directions

1. Prepare both cake mixes according to the directions on the back of the box. *Bake half of the cake mix into one large bread loaf pan, and the other in an 9" x 9" pan.*

2. Remove cakes from pans and let cool.

3. Place bread pan cake in center of serving tray.

4. *Place 9" x 9" cake on cutting board. Cut four 1½-inch strips from cake.*

5. *Cut a triangle off one of the corners of the 9" x 9" cakes. Set aside.*

6. Place the two-inch strips lengthwise on either side of the loaf.

7. Place the triangle piece on the front of the cake, as shown in the diagram. Place some extra cake on top of the triangle to produce a slight bump for the head.

8. Fill in any gaps with leftover pieces of cake.

9. Place the frosting in a bowl and dye to desired color. Frost the rat entirely.

10. Use candies to build a face on the rat. Stick the licorice in the back end for a tail.

11. Add pupils on eyes and outline of rat's legs with black decorating gel.

Utensils

Bread loaf pan
9" x 9" pan
Knife
Serving tray
Frosting utensils

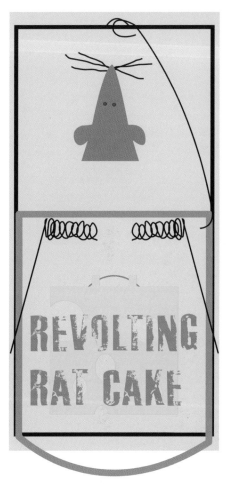

Ingredients

2 strawberry cake mixes
(Two 18.25 oz/517g)
Ingredients to prepare mixes
2 cans vanilla cream cheese
frosting (Two 16 oz/454g)
Food coloring
Various candies for face, paws
Licorice for tail
1 tube black decorating gel

SEA SLIME SANDWICHES

Difficulty: 2
Grossness: 1
Serves: 4

Directions

1. Cut the cookie dough into 8 evenly-shaped portions. Roll the dough into balls and place on cookie sheet. *Bake as directed on package.*

3. Put softened vanilla ice cream in freezer-safe bowl. Mix in blue food coloring until ice cream becomes the desired color and add ¾ gummy candies.

4. Refreeze the ice cream for 30 minutes. Take it out of the freezer and spoon the ice cream onto 4 cookies and place the other 4 cookies on the top.

5. Push the remaining gummy candies around the outside of ice cream. If you like, serve in a beach bucket and decorate with crushed graham crackers for sand.

step 3

Ingredients

1 package pre-made chocolate chip cookie dough (18 oz/510g)
3 cup vanilla ice cream, softened
Blue food coloring
Various sea creature candies and gummies—octopi, fish, green sour string (kelp)
4 graham crackers, crushed (optional)

Utensils

Cookie sheet
Freezer-safe bowl
Beach bucket (optional)

SEVERED ARM CAKE

Ingredients

1 package angel food cake mix (16oz/454g)
Ingredients to prepare mix
¼ cup powdered sugar
1 quart (1L) strawberry sherbet, softened
1 tablespoon lemon juice
1½ teaspoon cornstarch
2 pirouette cookie sticks
½ cup strawberry ice cream sauce
Several strands of licorice whip

Utensils

15" x 10" jelly roll pan
Clean linen kitchen towel
Wire rack
Plastic wrap
Serving tray
Spoon
Fake plastic hand (glove stuffed with cotton balls will also work)

step 3

step 5

Directions

1. Prepare cake batter according to directions. Line a 15" x 10" jelly roll pan with waxed paper. Pour the batter into pan. Bake at 350 degrees for 20 minutes, or until cake bounces back when touched.

2. Lay a clean linen towel on a flat surface and sprinkle with ¼ cup powdered sugar. *Dump cake onto towel, peel off wax paper, and use towel to roll cake.* Sit cake seam down on wire rack for 30 minutes.

3. *Carefully unroll cake on towel.* Spread softened frozen yogurt on top of cake, spreading it to the edges. Reroll cake.

4. *Wrap roll tightly with plastic wrap.* Freeze for at least 3 hours.

5. Place jelly roll on serving platter, leaving room to place the hand on the end of the platter later. Break pirouette candies in half. Dip broken ends in strawberry sauce and stick into the end of jelly roll, raspberry-dipped ends out, for broken bones.

6. Cut licorice whips into two-inch pieces and stick into roll near broken bones. Spoon strawberry sauce around the bones and wound.

7. Stick fake hand at end of the platter opposite the bones and freeze until ready to serve.

Ingredients

1 chocolate cake mix (18.25 oz/454g),
  plus ingredients to make cake
2 Twinkies
1 can chocolate frosting (16 oz/454g)
1 package chocolate sandwich
  cookies (18 oz/510g)
3 Milano cookies

Utensils

9" X 13" cake pan
Frosting spatula
Small plastic skeleton

GRAVEYARD
CAKE

and place on serving platter.

2. Cut off the bottom half of two Twinkies and place on cake for grave mounds.

3. *Create a coffin out of graham crackers, stuck together with frosting.* Set on cake.

4. Cut coffin-sized hole in cake. Remove extra cake and place coffin in hole. Make a coffin "lid" out of another piece of graham cracker and place into cake, ajar, next to coffin.

5. Frost cake, including Twinkies and lid.

6. *Pipe R.I.P. on Milano cookies.* Break off edges as shown in the picture. Stick cookies askew into graveyard at the heads of twinkie and coffin graves. Use frosting to secure.

7. Crush chocolate sandwich cookies *in a food processor* or with a rolling pin, as shown on page 45, step 2.

8. Sprinkle crumbs over graveyard, with a larger pile next to coffin cover, as if dirt had recently been displaced.

9. Insert plastic skeleton into coffin. Serve.

Difficulty: 4
Grossness: 2
Serves: 12

step 4

step 4

step 5

PARTY IDEAS

ALTHOUGH MOST OF THE RECIPES IN THIS BOOK ARE SUITABLE FOR A HALLOWEEN PARTY, THE DESSERTS CAN SERVE AS CENTERPIECES FOR OTHER THEMED PARTIES, BIRTHDAY PARTIES, AND SCOUT ACTIVITIES.

Pirate Party (Severed Arm Cake)

- Plan a treasure hunt.
- Give gold pieces, plastic jewels, and pirate flags.
- Wear hooks, eye patches, and pirate hats.
- Make telescopes out of paper towel rolls and pirate hats out of construction paper.
- Create treasure map invitations.

Astronaut/Space Party (Alien Cupcakes)

- Let children make their own alien cupcakes and eat astronaut ice cream.
- Hang glow-in-the-dark stars, have lights dimmed, or use Christmas or black lights.
- Wear sashes that have a NASA emblem and say "Astronaut in Training."
- Play "Pin the Eyeball on the Alien."
- Start a Draw-an-Alien contest.
- Cover walls in black fabric or butcher paper.
- Decorate the ceiling with helium balloons.

Western Party (Cow Pie Cake)

- Play horseshoes.
- Give out cowboy hats, bandanas, and licorice "ropes."
- Hang reward posters of the guest of honor.
- Decorate with hay bales and red checked tablecloths.
- Stage a Wild West gunfight with water guns.

Medical Themed Party (Bleeding Brain)

- Freeze water in a surgical glove and float in punch.
- Invite guests to come dressed as nurses or doctors.
- Provide doctors' masks or hats at the door.
- For party favors, give bandages and syringe pens.
- Serve drinks in test tubes and food in petrie dishes.

Bug Party (Bug and Dirt Cake)

- Give magnifying glasses, bug nets and gummy worms.
- Go on a bug hunt. The guest who finds the most wins.
- Scatter plastic bugs on the table.
- Wear antennae.

Housewarming Party (Bathroom Bar)

- Decorate with rubber duckies
- Have guests come in bathrobes.
- Provide a soap-making station.

Hillbilly Party: (Road Kill Cheesecake)

- Buy sets of teeth that are blacked out or stick out at odd angles, or blacken your teeth with eyeliner.
- Dress in plaid, jeans, and overalls.
- Play Bluegrass music.
- Learn square dancing for entertainment.
- Find junk from your garage or local thrift store to hang around the party area.